THE FIRST
365

THE FIRST

365

HOW TO SIGN FOUR-FIGURE CLIENTS OVER THE PHONE FROM ANYWHERE IN THE WORLD

AARON BRANCH

You are just one call away
from $2000 to $4000.

Dedicated to Holly, my fiancée,
who has supported me in my
life, career, and sacrifices.

I would not have survived
'The First 365' without you.

CONTENTS

INTRODUCTION......1

CHAPTER ONE   **WHY JUMP?**......5
MY STORY: SPORTING BEGINNINGS......5
MY STORY:
THE DECISION......8
MY STORY:
THE WINDOW OF OPPORTUNITY......10
WHAT ARE YOUR OPTIONS?......12
BEING YOUR OWN BOSS......14
THE LEGACY......16
BUSINESS WILL NEVER DIE......19
EXERCISE: THE VISION BOARD......20

CHAPTER TWO   **CHANGING LANES (AND FUEL)**......23
THREE-LANE MOTORWAY......23
CHANGE: OUR GREATEST OBSTACLE......25
ENERGY......28
ROUTINE......29

CHAPTER THREE   **SURVIVAL OVER EVERYTHING**......33
MY STORY: SUBOPTIMAL LIFE......33
BEING RESOURCEFUL......34
OPTIMISING LIFE......36
RELAPSES......37

CHAPTER FOUR   **DON'T GET TOO HIGH**......45
EARLY WINS......46
VICTORY HYPNOSIS......49

CHAPTER FIVE   **NOTHING IS PROMISED**......51
MY STORY: REALITY CHEQUE......51
THE POWER OF NOW......53
ATTACHMENT......56

CHAPTER SIX   **MAKE YOUR BUSINESS
THE BEST IT CAN BE**......61

CHAPTER SEVEN **THE HUNT, THE CHASE, THE KILL**.................65
PROSPECTING – THE HUNT...............................66
FIRST CONTACT SCRIPT.....................................68
PITCHING - THE CHASE.......................................71
PRE-CALL..71
FIVE STEPS TO A SOLID SALES CALL...............75
CLOSING ON YOUR OFFER – THE KILL........82
OBJECTION HANDLING.....................................87

CHAPTER EIGHT **POSITIONING
AND PERSONAL BRANDING**...........91
MY STORY: BRANDING DAY..............................92
CONTENT...94
PLATFORMS...97
SOCIAL PROOF...98

CHAPTER NINE **GIVE YOURSELF THE BEST
OPPORTUNITY TO SUCCEED**..........101
AGENCY PARTNER PROGRAM.......................101
EVERYTHING I WISH I HAD..............................102
HOW CAN IT SERVE YOU?...............................104
THE DECISION..106

CHAPTER TEN **MY FIRST 365: THE BENTLEY CLIENT**...........107

TESTIMONIALS..113

INTRODUCTION

This book is for agency owners, entrepreneurs, wantrepreneurs, graduates, non-graduates, corporate workers and anyone else who is not satisfied with their current surroundings and income.

If you did everything you thought you were supposed to do, were told to do, even expected to do, but found there wasn't enough fulfilment or money at the end of the rabbit hole, continue reading. The information I am going to share with you in this book will revolutionise the way you look at business.

It is not a coincidence this book landed in your hands. There are no coincidences in life. I believe we all get exactly what we deserve, good and bad. In this case I can assure you the end result will be good for your income and impact on this planet.

I jumped headfirst into starting my own business, with all the excitement and pain that comes with it. I quickly realised that knowing and doing are universes apart. I researched extensively through my university years and continue to do so, but none of what I read would prepare me for the roller coaster of having a business and needing to make money to survive.

I now run a successful digital marketing agency helping businesses succeed in their sales growth goals. I also run a mentor program to help new businesspeople avoid making the same mistakes I did when I was setting out, and shortcut to the success I have now.

In this book I will guide you through your first 365 days in business. I will also recount some of my experiences and perspectives for the benefit of anyone who might find themselves in similar situations. It is not pretty. I want this to serve as a powerful tool in every start-up business owner's arsenal as they grow, enrich and fulfil other people's lives through their work.

Consider this book your trusty companion. It will help you realise, "Shit, it wasn't just me."

Those mistakes were normal, those lessons were necessary, and the experience was the most valuable thing we gained from it.

In the second half of the book, I will set out practical examples of how you can generate opportunities (leads) and turn them into paying clients using social media and a single phone call.

I don't pretend to know everything about marketing and you might disagree with my views. I welcome your objections. I will probably disagree with myself and this book in years to come as I continue to grow. But the foundation of my real-world education is written in this book.

This is not a laborious, literary book. I am not a professional writer, though I do enjoy writing. This book is here to help the people who recognise there may be a better option through starting their own business, and want to be prepared for certain experiences that were not highlighted enough when I prepared for the great leap into entrepreneurship.

This is the first 365!

CHAPTER ONE

WHY JUMP?

MY STORY: SPORTING BEGINNINGS

My motivation when starting my business, like so many others, was money.

The straw that broke the camel's back was the recruiting job I took in Canary Wharf after turning down four professional basketball contracts in Europe.

My background was entirely in basketball throughout my education. I was lucky enough to leave the UK when I was 19 and compete on scholarships in Toronto and Chicago. I returned to a scholarship at London South Bank University when I was 21.

My goal was always to be a professional basketball player like many of my teammates. It was only when I graduated that I realised what my value on the European basketball market was. I remember the day I called up two ex-teammates who were in the German Regionalliga League and told them what I was offered. Both said they began on similar or worse salaries. I couldn't believe it. My world was flipped on upside down.

Two of the offers came from a month-long recruitment camp in Barcelona with an organisation called the European Basketball Academy. I used the money I had left over from university scholarships and bursaries to fund my stay.

One coach came down from Croatia. His name was Martin Blaho, and we had been told he was on a tight budget. He was a great coach. We ran through some great drills and sessions with him. After coaching us for two days, he wanted to take measurements. He measured our height, weight, wingspan, chest size, palm size and shoe size. Then he asked everyone who had been measured a question I'll never forget: "What is the absolute minimum you will take to begin your pro career?"

One by one he went through the squad mainly made up of players from the United States. When he got to me, I said I was a graduate from the UK and was confident I could get a job for at least £24,000 back home. I said I would take €1500 Euros - approximately £1350 - a month. Blaho acknowledged my answer. What came next blew me away.

A young Polish point guard was next in line for the same question. He said he would play for €200 a month.

That's €2000 for a 10-month season, if they pay you on time or at all. This player was not stupid, he was well-educated and spoke good English. I was disgusted at the state of the European Basketball market. It is a buyers' market. There are so many players desperate for a spot on a roster to pursue their dream, they are being extorted to begin their careers.

But the real underlying concern is this: if they don't take the €200 contract, what would they do instead? For most of the players I met, the answer was "Not much."

Later, I confronted the Polish player in the rehabilitation pool. (Mentally I definitely need it) I asked why he felt his value as a human being was only €200 a month. The story he told me about the economy in Poland clearly outlined the desperation of his self-evaluation. All power to him.

Personally, I would not even waste my time considering such a low salary. I come from a UK economy that competes in the top ten in the world, and I had never been so grateful for that until speaking to this Polish player.

I returned from Barcelona with offers in hand and a bitter, confused state of mind. My best offer was for €600 per month. I spent two weeks agonising over my decision. "Should I just take it? I've come this far. I should just see it through. What have I got to lose?"

MY STORY: THE DECISION

My final decision was one of the most difficult I have made in my life. I politely declined every offer. I couldn't shake off one important fact: For the lifestyle I want to live, €600 would not be enough.

I also didn't want to commit to being in a foreign country for 10 months a year with no investment potential, and there were no role models from the UK who had made a significant living off professional basketball.

I decided that if I was no longer going to compete on the court, I was going to compete in an office. I needed to find a company and industry with a commission structure suited to my finance-driven needs. I found a role through a recommendation with a recruitment agency in Canary Wharf.

I went to London for the first interview. I was so focused, so self-assured. I wanted the opportunity to perform and was ready to pitch my skill set like a beast.

The man interviewing me would end up becoming my mentor. He told me he wanted me to meet the Managing Director the following week. In this meeting I would pitch something to him. When I told him a competing firm had just made me an offer, he moved my second interview to the following day. That meant another day in London, in the same suit, shirt and boxers. I managed to borrow a pair of socks from a friend and put on a new tie to try and freshen things up. This wasn't ideal, but sometimes you have to get in the trenches (not the best analogy for underwear, I know). Within two weeks of the second interview I was employed with a salary of £24,000 and a seat at the table.

Three months later I had billed nearly £20,000 for the company, all the while polishing up my business skills. Every day I was pitching, closing, organising and creating. It was a 360 role at its finest, and absolute dog work at its most common. I gained valuable insights from the role and had a well-seasoned boss and mentor tugging on my leash.

But it wasn't to last. My ambition and insatiable need to have more continued to interrupt the working relationships between me and my superior. The final straw was when he told me I would only get 5 percent commission because I was still on my three-month probation. I never went back after that call.

Working in Canary Wharf was the least fulfilling time of my entire life. Which is why it didn't last any longer than three months. I used to walk to the office, which took around 30 minutes every morning. I could have caught the tube, but I needed the fresh air before spending over 10 hours in the office. My thoughts were clearest on these walks. I knew what I had to do to get out of the situation, and I knew I could not let a career in recruitment be my legacy.

Telling my boss I wouldn't be continuing the role meant sacrificing my impending commissions. I realised many companies keep their employees from leaving, using their hard-earned commissions as ransom. It wasn't enough to keep me. Hell no. I had bigger fish to fry.

I now had no job and no income. I spent several days meditating on my next actions.

MY STORY: THE WINDOW OF OPPORTUNITY

It was my girlfriend Holly who eventually gave me the nudge to go out on my own.

"What better time could there be for you to start a business?" she asked.

She was right. The window of opportunity to start a business is narrower than most people think. Once responsibilities and dependencies kick in, the risk of going it alone grows massively. When I started my business I had no kids and no mortgage, two factors that can influence every decision someone makes.

Think about this question. Let her words serve you as they served me. "What better time could there be for you to start a business?"

If you are already rocking your way up the entrepreneurial ladder, then take pleasure in knowing you are one of the very few who have. There are more employees than employers in the world. Employers provide opportunity and value by taking the risk to plug into the game of business.

There is no time like the present. If there is something holding you back and you still have an excuse for why you shouldn't do something right now to change your circumstances, here are a few questions I considered in the days before I committed:

Do you believe in yourself?

One thing I have developed from achieving many of my goals in sport is a lot of self-belief. This is the core component that has driven my commitment. I knew I could make a success of anything I put my mind to, and so can anyone else who has the right characteristics.

What is your risk appetite?

How does the worst-case scenario make you feel? If you started a business and lost it all, all the luxuries you have acquired could get thrown straight out the window. Business can bleed you dry. How comfortable are you with that thought? If you have little to lose then you may not care about falling flat on your face. But if you are attached to your lifestyle, you might want to step back and evaluate how much you can afford to lose.

How bad do you want it?

I know people who would sell their own grandmother if it helped them achieve their business goals. I also know people who cringe at the thought of overcoming challenges I have encountered on my journey. But in the end, if you are to take the plunge into business, it will boil down to how bad you want it. "Kinda wanting it" isn't going to compel you to action.

As humans we are programmed to stay in our comfort zones, to do what is easy first. To come home from work, sit on the sofa and stare at a screen almost motionless for our two hours of "freedom". To buy products that we would never want if it wasn't for advertising. That isn't life. For me, life is about connection, emotion and love whilst experiencing new environments, cultures and people (and of course a couple hours per week on netflix).

WHAT ARE YOUR OPTIONS?

It is important to understand your own reasons for wanting to start a digital marketing agency. What first caught your attention?

For me it was the talk of freedom, being your own boss, flexibility and the abundance that having a successful business would bring. All these ideas, although true, are interesting to reflect on after your first 365 days in business.

Here is a less optimistic depiction of those benefits and how I see them now:

Freedom: The freedom to be broke if you don't work very hard to find and execute sales opportunities. The freedom to be chewed up and spit back out by the competitive world of business along with over 90 percent of all start-ups.

Being your own boss: "No one can tell me what to do," I said while fantasising about how many clients I would sign in month one. Yes, you are your own boss, but now you either have customers or clients to please, or even better, both! And before they even give you the opportunity to please them, you must convince them you have the most valuable and least risky option to solve their problem. Not easy when your only case study is one project you delivered for a company you no longer work with because they went bust ("Ahem, but we had nothing to do with that…").

Flexibility: Yes, you will be flexible with your time. You can go home early and you can wake up late, all at the cost of you and your business probably amounting to nothing. The flexibility to walk your dog whenever you like has been a perk I have enjoyed at times. Anything else is under the scrutiny of my conscience and unfulfilled sales targets. One thing that becomes extremely precious is your time. More flexibility is a dangerous aphrodisiac for starting a business.

Abundance: I firmly believe entrepreneurs can achieve this. Abundance can be in anything. The abundance I have built is in relationships, new people in my network, experiences, personal development and fulfilment, to name a few. But there is also an abundance of struggle, doubt, fear and hardship. This is just part of the package. Every entrepreneur, owner and consultant I know can recall a handful of times where they were overrun and looked longingly back at the safety net of their previous jobs.

BEING YOUR OWN BOSS

Freedom. When I was employed in Canary Wharf my work shifts were 8am to 7pm in the office. On paper, the work hours were 9am to 6pm, but anyone leaving before 7pm would be frowned upon.

At 5.50pm I would look around to see anyone twitch towards grabbing their coat. Some people would perform rituals before they left. Organising their desks, taking their dirty mugs to the kitchen, even putting on their

Bluetooth headsets for a call and pacing up and down the room scouting out an exit strategy.

As stupid as this sounds, it was the reality. I hated it with a vengeance. I wasn't free and that was a very big problem for me. One day on my way to work, while listening to a song by Pharrel Williams called "Freedom", I realised I wasn't free. This was a key driver for my eventual escape.

Being your own boss might seem like your true calling. "I wasn't born to work for someone else. I can do it all on my own. I can be the one on the top of the food chain giving vision and direction."

The only problem with that is you will most likely be your only employee when you start out.

I now have the privilege of sending information to my own staff. But, in the first 365 days, I wrote out orders and put them on my own desk to execute.

There is no hiding from the hard work, and it will make you question your fortitude and beliefs. When you have done over eight hours on the phone and don't have a single warm lead to show for it, that is when you really understand what pressure is. Extend that to a month and you start to doubt the validity of your business.

Nevertheless, there are always glimmers of hope to keep you pushing forward. You manage to patch up the wounds and stop the bleeding. Re-energise, strategize and execute. That's what being your own boss is all about. It's learning in the field and adapting to your environment. That means adapting your business, products and services to what the market needs, not what you think it needs.

Having the discipline to manage yourself is one of life's biggest challenges, whether you are in business or not. It takes tons of vision and effort to make yourself the best employee you will ever find. You will know you are on the right track when you can consistently say that about yourself.

You have to be the hardest working person in your business for it to manage those heavy hits that you take in year one. Unless you are at the front pushing through and over those waves of doubt, failure and fear, you will get washed away like 90 percent of start-ups inevitably do.

THE LEGACY

Consider these questions: What will you leave behind? How will the world remember your contribution to it? I personally don't care about the legacy of my name. My legacy is the work and value I can add to people's lives and businesses.

As employees, our capacity to contribute is vastly undermined. I was restricted by my roles with limited autonomy to decide what I could take on.

But as an employer, I have a different set of rules to play by. We employers can create and adjust our position in the world freely. The independence to make those decisions lets us deliver the very best of ourselves and our work to the world, no matter what industry it is in.

My legacy is not about being rich. It's about developing multigenerational wealth. The type of wealth that is difficult to lose long after I'm gone. The wealth that only comes from the consistent results of helping people get what they want. Value driven wealth. Integrity driven ideas that make win-win situations in every deal and negotiation. Empowering people to profit from their passions, or even just to profit.

For some people, the art of making money is their passion. It fills them with excitement and joy. For others, winning in the game of business is more important.

Both are true for me. I get a rush of endorphins every time I close a deal. It reminds me of winning a close game in basketball. From the introduction to the completion of a deal, it is all about execution. The strategy, patience and trust you have to master to get to a position where you can win changes from deal to deal, game to game. I love the challenge of adjusting to your opponent, adjusting your game.

But in this world, I am not trying to beat my client. I am trying to make them my teammate. I find it much more fun to convince them to come over to my side and win together. I know if I bring over enough clients and win with them, my legacy will build itself.

So what will my legacy be? It is too early to tell. But when it is all said and done, I would like to be remembered as someone who didn't sell for the easy path; someone who challenged beliefs that were imprinted on me from a young age and dramatically shifted his way of thinking; someone who built his success on the shoulders of those he helped become more successful.

And finally, if I was to add one last thing to my legacy, it would be that I was a good father. I have no kids yet, but I want my greatest achievement to be raising the next generation in the best possible way I can.

Take a moment to think about your life. What will your legacy be? What will the people closest and furthest away from you remember you for? What was the energy that you shared with them in your interactions? What type of life did you lead?

These were all questions I answered for myself when I chalked up a vision for my future.

BUSINESS WILL NEVER DIE

One thing that I have always believed is that there will always be a need for solutions to problems. Therefore, there will always be a need for solution agents.

There will always be compensation, in one form or another, for these solutions. So I can say with confidence that business will never die.

There will always be opportunities for people to find a problem and create a solution. Those people are you and me.

One thing to be careful of is manufacturing solutions for problems that don't yet exist.

A massive downfall of young wantrepreneurs is that their ideas are so focused on being different and unique that they forget the very essence of why anything does well: it needs to solve a problem.

Creating is a beautiful thing, and some of the best inventions came long ahead of their time. An example of this is Leonardo da Vinci's sketches of a parachute. Around 500 years later, an inventor in France would look at these sketches to create and test the first parachute. Jumping off a cliff to test this invention in Da Vinci's day may have been premature. But now parachutes are common functional, and ubiquitous in air travel.

Getting into business doesn't require an original idea. There is a reason there are so many competitors in most industries. I work in digital advertising, and I cannot drive through any town or city centre without spotting a competitor.

But being in a competitive environment doesn't mean you can't compete. And that is why you must be clear about why you are in the game. Is it because you believe in your invention and yourself or is it that you hate the alternative? Whatever your reasons, you should take absolute confidence in the fact that business will always need new ideas and solutions from whoever is skilled and willing enough to put in their pound of flesh.

EXERCISE: THE VISION BOARD

Here is a brief exercise that I have done myself. I enjoy this, and it reminds me of the scale of what I am trying to achieve. It is all about helping you get clear on the lifestyle you want to live.

On my own vision board, I have kept the objects of desire strictly materialistic. This is because having my own Ferrari one day excites me. Having the house that I want to live in drives me to put my head down and go after it.

However, I don't want you to just print out images of the things you want. This requires some research. Go online and search for every item you want put onto your vision board as if you were looking to buy them. Pay close attention to the prices. Write them down on a post-it note. When you print the images and put them on your board (I recommend a cork board) put a post-it note on top of the image that tells you the actual cost of that item. This will shift your focus from the fantasy of what you want to the reality of how much that is going to cost. Understand how expensive that property would be. Feel how much money you would need for that car, boat, motorcycle, jet, or island.

Once you have your board with images and prices of things you are motivated and excited to have, place it somewhere you will see it every day. Mine sits on top of the whiteboard directly in front of my desk. I see it. I know the prices of those items like the back of my hand.

You might also like to include pictures of family and other non-material things. I initially tried this myself, but the vision board is not about the things money can't buy. I don't believe money can buy you love, loyalty or similar intangibles. This exercise is about the income you need to generate to live the life of your dreams.

CHAPTER TWO

CHANGING LANES (AND FUEL)

THREE-LANE MOTORWAY

Think about it like this. When you get into business you are on a three-lane motorway. We are all on the same road but that doesn't mean we are going at the same speed. The car you are overtaking is your "less optimal self". The bad-habit, unfocused, lazy and more negative version of yourself. That version of you, V1, isn't going anywhere fast. V1 is in the slow lane.

To overtake, you put your foot down and burn more fuel. You pass V1 with ease. Now you're cruising. You're enjoying the scenes around you. There is so much going on. You've got your music playing. Your phone on your lap in case you get a text message, and you are daydreaming about what you're going to do when you "make it". There isn't much traffic in front of you. You look in the rear-view mirror and V1 is nowhere to be seen.

You barely have time to see someone screaming up behind you in the right lane. You never noticed it approaching because you were so distracted. It's V3, baby! Flying past so fast you barely have the chance to notice that it's you.

You thought you were doing well because of how poor V1 was. But as V2 you are probably still below standard. What are your standards?

Look at your everyday life. What you wear, eat and drive. How you speak, feel and treat others. These are all a part of your standards. They are completely subjective and custom to you. No one can tell you how high or low your standards are because they don't have your perspective.

But when you see V3 flying past, you know you're not where you could be. V3 is optimal, high performance and most importantly full of fuel and energy. V3 has none of the distractions V2 has. While you were busy admiring yourself for passing V1, V3 hadn't even left the house. But when V3 got on the road, it went straight past you to the same destination. That all comes down to a focus on energy and being optimal.

To change lanes, you're going to need a lot of energy. Energy to break habits. Energy to mute distractions. Energy to resist temptation. Everyday I try to get more energy.

Keep your eye on which lane you are travelling in. It is important to understand where you are. Are you in the right state of mind to overtake the weaker versions of yourself?

I know a lot of people who are interested in the fast lane, but they don't have enough energy in the tank to drive the necessary speed. Not yet anyway.

Remember not to settle for V3; V4 and V5 are on the way!

CHANGE: OUR GREATEST OBSTACLE

Change is probably one of the most important parts of life because it applies to everything. Work, friends, family, business, spirituality, knowledge and so on. All things change.

Unconsciously or consciously we change our ideas. Something that is important to me today may mean nothing to me in five months.

The hardest thing I have ever had to change is myself and my habits. My business would never have been born without change. I would never have met many of my clients without change. So much would be different if I never made some dramatic changes.

And it is not just our habits that are hard to change. But what about our goals, targets and dreams. It can be very difficult to convince someone to aim high if they have been taught their whole life that they could never achieve. It is usually just as difficult to influence them to take a direction they have never taken before. I went through this.

From the age of 16 it was my only goal to make it in basketball. I dedicated years of my energy to the sport, emotionally and physically. Spiritually, even. Basketball was my God. I studied it, practised it and loved it. I went to North America for two years in pursuit of better skills, competition and opportunity. I was so sharply focused on achieving my goals that if anyone mentioned an alternative to a professional career in basketball, I shot them down instantly. I was going to be a pro and that was the end of it.

But I was not prepared to take the low pay I was offered, or to value myself as a human being in the beginners' bracket that those teams put me in. I was grateful but very disappointed. It was time for a change.

I turned down the pro offers and accepted that to live the lifestyle I wanted, basketball was far too high a risk to take. I had equipped myself with business knowledge throughout my life, and I was very confident my earning capacity would be realised sooner in business than in basketball.

I advise anyone who is not thriving in their work and life to consider change. Deeply consider stepping into the unknown. Have faith in your habits to deliver you results in any industry you apply yourself to. You are the only person accountable for your earning capacity.

We are in an age where information is available at the click of a button for free. Harnessing that information to bring value to people could be your opportunity to make a huge positive impact in your own life and others. Just because you haven't considered an idea yet, doesn't mean that it is not there. You just have to be ready to change for it when it arrives.

What about those who condemn change? "You changed," they say. My response is "You didn't."

To evolve we must change and adapt. Get better, stronger and more skilled. To end this passage, I'd ask you to ponder something a great mentor once shared with me:

"To get everything that you want, who do you need to become?"

ENERGY

Energy is universal. It is everything we see, feel, touch and think. It is the great decider. Who can maintain their energy at the highest level consistently to thrive in their competitive arena?

Everything we do in life either gives or takes energy. Every action we take impacts our energy.

Consider short-term energy and long-term energy. Going to the gym and expending your short-term energy until you are physically fatigued will aid you in the future when you want to go longer than you currently can. That is a long-term energy positive.

I boost my short-term energy using breathing exercises, meditation and walks with my dogs.

When I first began working in my single cubicle trying to build a business. I thought of every minute as gold dust. I would not leave the room except for bathroom breaks and food. It was like a prison cell. The room was slightly wider than my arm span and just a few metres long. The worst thing was the tiny window. Low natural light was a killer to my energy. I would leave that room each day more exhausted than necessary because I had a short-term energy deficit.

As if starting a business and trying to get your first clients on board isn't hard enough. Particularly on my lonesome in a single room with a phone and a laptop. Lack of natural light was the icing on the cake. It wasn't healthy. I told myself this was how it had to be, that I should be uncomfortable, that it should be tough. That thought was stupid.

Don't make things harder than they need to be, ever. There is no need. I had thought that spending all my time with my head down would get the most done. But I realised this was not the most optimal way to work.

I was thirsty for some energy boosters. I decided to break my day up by taking walks near my office. I would do this at least twice a day just to get some light and air. Rain or sun I would put my red North Face jacket on and start walking. Sometimes this walk was as simple as going to the Tesco supermarket to grab something.

After walking back in the office, I could clearly focus on where to put my energy. I immediately started getting more done.

Something as simple as a walk, some light and some air can make all the difference. Clarity is everything.

ROUTINE

Routine is an area which is highly up for debate.

Some argue that having everything scheduled in your day is the best way to get the most done. Others argue that being flexible and adaptive lets you get the most important things done. Either way, it's getting shit done that counts.

I have heard enough analysis to last a lifetime. People talk and analyse things in extreme depth to avoid doing them. "I can't do that until this, this and this happens."

Your routine should promote taking action.

I wake up at 7am most days, eat, shit, shave. Then I head to work. By work I mean my laptop and phone, whether that be in my kitchen, my home office, the car, the office I have in Birmingham or the office I have in London. Any one of these works. As a digital consultant, I can work anywhere I have an internet connection.

My work routine varies, but I have always been strict about scheduling things into my calendar. That's for business and my personal life: if it's not in my calendar I just won't make it, given all the other things I have going on in the business.

Between handling clients, proposals consultants, prospects et cetera, there usually is no finish line in sight. Being an ex-athlete, this is something I'm used to. I have been mentally tuned for performance. This means that when developing my skills, I try to always push myself to the boundaries of discomfort before giving up and giving in.

My routine flexes and bends to the goals and needs of each day. Some days I work, exercise, sleep or eat less. This is something you need to be prepared for if you want to see a lasting change in your first 365.

CHAPTER THREE

SURVIVAL OVER EVERYTHING

MY STORY: SUBOPTIMAL LIFE

After starting my agency, the first thing to abandon me was my fitness and eventually my physically fit and able body. During my time as an athlete I would burn upwards of 5000 calories every day through gym and basketball sessions. I was driven to have my body in the peak performance state to gain an edge on the court. When I turned down my offers to continue professional basketball my reason for working out also left me. I just didn't have the motivation or logical reason to get into the gym.

But there was something else missing, which I had taken for granted the entire time I was playing competitive sport. It was my coaches and teammates. They were a great source of inspiration for every workout and training session. They were there constantly pushing me, directly or subconsciously, to become something better. This is something I realised and acted on in my business.

How much was not having a mentor or a coach costing my business? How much more could I grow with the right people around me pushing me towards my targets? This eventually led me to the most influential action I have ever attributed any of my success to: reaching out to mentors and asking to pay for their services. This was truly humbling to do, and extremely rewarding once applied.

BEING RESOURCEFUL

One of the first things I needed to learn when starting this journey into agency life was being resourceful. The cost of doing business is not cheap. I call it the "cost of sale". Are you aware of the guaranteed costs to anticipate in your first year of business? Here's a list to consider:

Laptop/computer: You're going to need some processing power to manage the hundreds of internet browser tabs open every day. Will you deliver all the client work yourself? There are tonnes of resources online to help you do that without taking up huge amounts of memory on your computer. Research what sort of processing power is needed for your industry.

Mobile phone: If you don't have one, you need one. In addition to your existing handset you may need to look at adding international minutes to your plan for international client calls.

Transport: Whether the budget for transport goes to your vehicle or public transport, you need to factor it in. I personally recommend and teach closing deals over the phone, but the opportunity to meet clients face-to-face is sometimes an advantage. Remember to have some collateral prepared for those first months of business to help you get around.

Advertising spend: That's correct. When you are beginning this does not have to be huge, but having a small budget to promote your posts on pay-to-play platforms such as Facebook and Instagram is essential if you want to fast-track your impact and brand growth.

Those are a few costs to think about. There will be more along the way. Survival is the name of the game in your first six months of digital agency life.

There is no getting around it. You need money to come into your business. To make money and meet your costs, you must begin your journey of mastery around lead generation and sales. We have broken down strategies and tactics to doing this in a step-by-step program in our Social Media Marketing Network Online Courses. More on this later.

For now I want you to simply consider the first and most important truth you will come to know in business: sales equals survival.

OPTIMISING LIFE

Trying to become the best version of yourself is a constant grind filled with overwhelming effort and discomfort. If I look at my own journey, I recall a very different version of myself throughout my teens and early twenties when the success of a basketball career went very quickly to my head.

When optimising your life, you need a very strong understanding of yourself, your strengths and your weaknesses. If you have never done an assessment on your personality, I recommend visiting 16personalities. com - this is something we complete with every student and mentee at the beginning of their program. The personality test is never 100 percent accurate, but you will likely find one or two pieces of feedback from it hyper relevant to your own life. You can then learn how to respond to situations and avoid emphasising your weaknesses.

The first way to optimise your life is through focusing on your weaknesses. Be critical and enjoy the process of preparing yourself for situations where you would previously have tripped up because you were ignorant to your behaviour patterns.

Don't dismiss this powerful step in optimisation. If I had taken this test earlier, I may have had more fun securing my first deals. That is important.

The next optimisation involves looking after some key areas to achieve balance. What makes up a human being? In no particular order, we are physical beings, spiritual beings, intellectual beings and emotional beings. Each of these aspects plays a part in the first year of your digital agency success, and you need to optimise each to succeed to your fullest.

RELAPSES

Stay away from anyone who is teaching you about the glory of agency life without accounting for the physical, mental and financial relapses you may experience on this journey.

The agency game will continually test you as you grow it. Whatever the phase of your journey you must prepare and anticipate the shit hitting the fan.

Let's break down the above categories and the fine balancing act that is agency growth and stability. I don't want to scare you too much. But I know you'll thank me for this later.

PHYSICAL:

Picture this: the long shift has begun. You're off the starting block. You're doing everything in your power to close your next deal to grow your business. Hours and hours of prospecting, meetings and proposal-building.

Couple that with the delivery of existing client work, project management, Facebook ads build, launch and management, and everything else that goes into having a successful agency business. What do you become?

You are working yourself to death. All you hear is "Hustle!" in a sharp, borderline annoying, Gary Vee voice. Every time you open social media you perceive people to be doing better than you, which leads you to even more "hustle" and "acquisition of knowledge," as Tai Lopez would say.

The above scenario is something I want to help you avoid. If you become physically drained, you will lose sight of everything. Endless working becomes a vicious cycle. Productivity isn't directly associated with time spent working. Don't make that mistake.

Please don't misunderstand me here. I am all for working eight-hour days in an optimised scheduled fashion. It is the lifeblood of what has helped us clear the revenue we have. You have to show up and you have to put in the time. But wasting time doing low-leverage tasks will not help you grow.

Here are a few pointers to keep you from going insane that I wish I knew and practised in the first 365 of starting my agency:

Walk outside at least twice a day. Once before you start working, either in your garden or on your street or even on your way to the office. Spend time breathing in some fresh air and cleansing your mind ready for the day ahead. At lunch, get out of your workspace at home or in the office and recharge your batteries. I know it is hard to justify when you have so much to do, but neglecting to reset your mind twice a day will destroy you. Clarity is everything.

Stay hydrated. Simply surviving isn't thriving. Your body is a performance vehicle and water as its primary need. Start the day with a 2-litre bottle of water next to your workstation. The bottle should be in sight, and you should drink a minimum of two bottles of water per day.

This game will dehydrate you senseless. The amount of energy it takes to run your agency will take its toll. Speaking on the phone, writing emails and building proposals is physical work. If you follow the strategies in my courses and training programs you will know that even more so. Keep the blood flowing freely. As the great martial artist Bruce Lee said: "Be like water."

Don't comfort eat or drink! I am guilty of this even to this day. The daily struggle to not overeat and reward myself for my hard work with food at my desk is real. If you are anything like me, you enjoy the gratification of the salt, sugar and fat-loaded products that sit on our shelves. It's no excuse to fall victim. The meal deal of a sandwich, crisps and fizzy drinks will slowly deteriorate your energy and keep you from being your best self. Without a manager to see your grind and tell you "Well done," it can become a habit to reward yourself at lunch. There is only one solution I have found to this: preparing my own food as often as possible.

A balanced diet is difficult when you are looking at your options in a supermarket. There is too much temptation and when you are yet to feel a win for the day it's easy to fall victim. Couple that with a cheeky pint of alcohol after work a couple of nights a week, and you're definitely heading in the wrong direction.

So, in a nutshell: clear your mind, stay hydrated and avoid fast food and alcohol.

What if I told you the actual cost to your business of bad physical health was a minimum of $15,000 in new business per year? Would you be more motivated? What if lacking energy costs you 150K per year? That literally could be what is on the line. Look after your physical form.

MENTAL:

Have you heard of escapism? Movies, Netflix, nights out, eating out, drinking, social media binges, gambling, console gaming, you name it. Doctors tell us the above will not have a seriously negative effect on us if practised in moderation. But all these things come with risks when abused or overdone. Depending on your personality, each of the above activities might appeal to you more or less.

When you are locked into your business growth you will experience times where all you want to do is "unplug". I dropped into several of these activities after working 10 to 12-hour days. I would find excuses to go out with friends, come home and order takeaways, and drinking alcohol became a routine activity.

It is normal and fine to enjoy some of these activities. Awareness to how much this affects you mentally is key.

Too much of anything can birth an addiction. Addiction can birth reliance. Reliance can create disasters.

What would happen if someone took away your Netflix, drinking, or social media? Would you still be able to operate at a high level and enjoy your day? Or are you leaning on these activities a little too much? I know I was.

Depending on where you are in your agency growth, your workload will differ. As you scale past $20K per month you should also benefit from more autonomy and team support. This is something I delve into extensively in my Agency Partner Program.

Keep your mindset clean and it will keep you clean. A great way to keep on the straight and narrow is to start a journal.

Write your true feelings in this as if no one will ever read it. Be specific and log what you're working on, and more importantly where it is going and why you are doing it. After writing an entry skip back to an earlier entry, and you will usually feel good about how far things have come for you.

This is something I practice myself when inspiration hits. I do not do this daily. I'd rather be writing an email to a client asking for payment than my feelings. But I can't dismiss how powerful it is to deeply express your feelings and emotions. Without keeping these at the forefront of your agency you might fall victim to thinking addiction is the cure to the hard work you endure.

FINANCIAL:

Stop for a second. Take a deep breath and lock into this section to avoid losing thousands of your earnings. Literally.

Let's say you're physically in check and mentally all good. You're focused and feeling good. Great. That's exactly where you want to be. Living the good life, baby!

Now you close your first substantial amount of business. What do you do? If you are one of my mentees you would probably be earning between $3000 and $5000 with around two clients at this point. Generally speaking you'd feel quite good, but now what?

What are the financial strategies and plans you have in place to organise and utilise your newfound income? What do you do with that finance? If you have debt you probably want to clear that all off, right? But how much liquidity should you leave in the business?

I aimlessly neglected to ask myself these questions in the first year of my agency. But you are not going to make the same mistakes as me.

I bought a Mercedes with £13,000 in cash. Got a second car just for fun. I spent thousands on watches that I never wear. I went on shopping sprees with my partner spending money just for the sake of it.

I have come to understand that this behaviour is typical for someone like myself who wasn't born into wealth. Neither of my parents were wealthy, which meant there was no real financial education passed on. Around 90 percent of the population is in a similar situation. Is that going to be your excuse for burning what you earn? Don't let it be.

I speak of these times in my first year of agency money with embarrassment. I had no wealth ratios, a very limited understanding of credit and interest, and an even slower appreciation for how little I had actually accomplished. In your first year and all the years subsequent to your successful cash flow-producing agency please focus on the next word: investing.

Before investing, clear your immediate debts with interest. Once you are debt-free start putting cash from your agency into assets that will bring you a residual income each month. Property and financial trading are my weapons of choice alongside two side businesses that I invest in. Investing your income will help you avoid the strains of poor spending habits you may have grown up with.

When it comes to spending, be frugal. Don't earn money to show others you have it. Earn it to show others how it can be done in an ethical and scalable manner.

CHAPTER FOUR

DON'T GET TOO HIGH

It's very easy to get carried away with the victories you experience in your business, particularly the financial milestones. As you gain experience and practice what you have learnt, you may start generating a lot of income. The type of income you have never seen before. If you are one of our agency partners or mentees you will know that your earnings increasing is a direct result of the success you have brought to your clients' lives and businesses.

The finances will often come with an accompanying admiration from your clients who went from strangers to loving you in a short space of time. How long does this take? As long as it takes you to present results.

The higher the value you bring to the relationship, the more admiration you receive and often the bigger your ego shall inflate. It is natural. We are tribal creatures. We evolved as humans to seek acceptance. When we do something to help others the financial reward is easy to measure and maintain. But the emotional reward can get out of hand very quickly. In this chapter I will break down some of the mistakes I made so you don't do the same. Don't get too high.

EARLY WINS

Life is crazy. I have single-handedly nurtured over 150 agency owners from $0 to $2000-plus in a four-week cycle. This sometimes makes it painful to remember how long it took me to reach that same income.

As these consultants grow, I also see the changes in their persona. Those first "wins" of signing deals can take someone from the brink of self-destruction to cloud nine.

As my own business sales started to roll into the bank, they just as quickly rolled out. I began thinking about all the people who didn't think I could pull it off who I had proved wrong. Those close to me who never opposed my actions, but also never supported me when starting my business and quitting my job. It was a downward spiral.

You know you're in the wrong place spiritually when you start asking yourself how to prove you are better than people.

Do you feel like this right now? Have you got people in your life who haven't supported you or you feel secretly want you to fail? The toughest part is when those people are your own parents - as some of the consultants I have trained have experienced.

These temptations conflict with the main principles I try to teach my consultants: humility, compassion and truth. I teach them to never be like me, be better than me.

Money will not make you a bad person. It will simply make you more of what you already are. If you are an arrogant S.O.B, you will become worse. If you are a selfless leader, you will become better. I'm not here to tell you who you are; I just want to make you ask the question.

Money changes some things, but here are two things money should not change:

HOW YOU TREAT OTHERS:

Listen very carefully to what comes next. It might awaken some pretty controversial feelings within you. Having money does not make you better than anybody else. Revolutionary, I know!

I can't stand arrogance in a consultant. I've sat with some extraordinarily wealthy people through my business, both self-made and inherited, and I noticed something about all of them. They are only human. They have the same physical makeup and internal organs we all have. It might disappoint you to hear that many of them, compared to the stereotypes that you might have grown up with, are quite unexceptional. Nothing special.

Fortunately, moguls, magnates and influencers have been very compassionate and helpful to me, but that never made me think more of them than I did of myself. That "rich" image that we are sold on social media and in Hollywood movies usually depicts the fools of society. Those characters might be introducing you to behaviours that will sabotage you in the long run. Treat everyone with the same level of respect and you will usually get the same.

YOUR SELF-WORTH:

The number of mentees that come through our doors wanting to be more, earn more and live more is incredible. The small intricate consistencies between their nature and behaviour is fast becoming a fascination of mine. Because of sport and my achievements, I have always had a high opinion of who I am and what I can contribute to society. I have always felt that no matter what it is, if I put my mind to it I can be successful given the right amount of time. Unfortunately, this isn't the case for many.

Even with the right prospecting, sales script, positioning and case studies (all of which are available through the mentorship program) some people can't get out of their own limiting belief systems.

I have narrowed down the self-defeating thoughts to something that sounds like this: "Because I currently don't have financial stability or confidence I am not as good as others out there doing better than me." If this is how you feel, I would like to invite you to scrap it. But this is easier said than done.

How you feel about yourself should not be in proportion to the money you make. I could lose everything I have built and would still have the desire and confidence to go and earn it back. The only way that would work is if I felt good about who I am internally. If you don't have that confidence in yourself yet, you should consider coaching and mentoring. Seek advice from others and go out into the world to get healed of these limiting belief systems. Over the long term they will continue to trip you up.

VICTORY HYPNOSIS

Imagine moving around in a state where you are absolutely out of touch with reality. You are literally two deals away from being in the top 5 percent of earners in your country. Once you start having some victories in your marketplace for your clients, you can become out of touch. This is called victory hypnosis.

This state of hypnosis can serve you well. Now your belief systems around your income have been upgraded and as you progress through life, you should create a systematic process of continuing to "level up" in health, relationships and wealth. This isn't about the high life; this is about controlling your mindset and discipline when you are in the first year of your agency.

You can elevate your income to new heights by signing one or two clients. You can also just as easily fall from that cloud when those clients stop working with you. You may be under this hypnosis right now. Can you afford to lose your most valuable two clients in your business without changing your business or your lifestyle?

If you are like me, the volume of clients you are serving balances out the loss of any business. The only way you can stop yourself from relying on a few clients is to grow your client base. Victory hypnosis can stunt your growth if you do not realise that unless you are growing you are shrinking.

Wherever you are at with your agency, do not become complacent. Simple. You will most likely increase your earnings as you continue in business (especially after reading this book). Avoid allowing that increase to jeopardise your true potential income.

CHAPTER FIVE

NOTHING IS PROMISED

MY STORY: REALITY CHEQUE

When I had my first £9000 month I was living the high life, or at least I thought I was. Holidays were booked a day in advance, sometimes even on the same day. I over-paid for things that were not investments and ran around throwing money like it was a curse to hang on to it.

I was standing in my kitchen getting ready to go to Birmingham airport. The phone rang. It was a client. Un-scheduled calls usually mean something is wrong. I paused for a second and felt my mind go from zero to 100 thoughts per second. I decided to bite the bullet and answer.

"Aaron, we need to talk."

Shit. Bells started going off in my mind.

I was literally standing there looking at my suitcase as the client told me they would not be continuing with our services. In that exact moment I could see the £4000 retainer they had paid me over the past three months disappear into thin air.

I started thinking on my feet, grasping at straws to tie them back into the solutions they wanted. But the battle was already lost. I had oversold.

Something I often speak about is not promising too much to clients. When it comes to talking about results, you must practice being "specifically vague". You must know your KPIs, but in marketing there are no guarantees. You can have the perfect funnel on paper and all the results in the world for similar businesses, but until those results are realised for that specific client you should avoid promising the exact results.

I had oversold this client. The deal was too good for my agency and the results weren't flooding in as anticipated over the past couple of months. Now the invoice came into question. They weren't looking likely to pay it all. This is where I have coined the term "reality cheque". The funds I had received previously had already been allocated and I was banking on this payment. To be honest, I had already spent it in my mind and on my credit card.

I was looking at the suitcase for a trip that would no longer be feasible. As the call progressed and slowly fizzled out, I sunk to the ground. My heart was heavy. How would I tell my partner that we don't have the money?

This was in no way, shape or form the client's fault. Yes, they owed us the final month's invoice (which they eventually paid) but the truth was I needed a reality cheque. I was over-extended on luxuries I couldn't afford. I was living the high life prematurely and paying the cost for being way out of my depth. I was already going on a trip and taking seven days out from the business. On a normal month I could recover and replace that client if I made it my mission.

This leads me to a huge lesson for anyone reading this book. Don't spend funds that you haven't collected. With credit, overdrafts and loans, it is easy to get carried away thinking that no payment to your business will be late and you will stay in the green. If you are charging upfront, you also get used to being ahead of the payment schedules. But if you are paying your team at the end of the month this can lead to cash flow issues quickly if you are not on top of your finances and spending habits.

Don't overextend financially to the point where a big fat reality cheque slaps you in the face. It is not fun.

THE POWER OF NOW

Nothing is promised in agency life. I'm yet to meet an agency owner who has told me a client has been with them forever. Why would they be? Even if you are the very best, you have to accept you are not the only option. This can lead to stress or it can lead to relief depending on how you feel towards your clients.

You should continually practice staying in the moment. As entrepreneurs we can often get caught up in the future. The targets we are trying to reach; the funnel we are building to launch months ahead; the lead magnets we build that will at some point get us a sale; and although all of these tasks are powerful and productive in their own right, you can't dismiss the immediate actions needed to get your business into a healthy position.

I did this. Before getting mentors, when leads were hard to come by, I started finding excuses to not do the hard things in my business. I spent my time planning and strategizing the most attractive plan on paper, and avoiding simply contacting businesses and booking appointments to pitch them.

And then there was the ultimate productivity killer: YouTube. I absolutely love YouTube. One video I made on the platform for promoting event marketing through Facebook Ads has delivered at least five clients for my agency. But that was me as a producer of content. That was very productive and produced a return on investment.

The danger of YouTube is when you start binge watching, looking for answers to questions you haven't even asked. Suggested videos can lead you to a place that looks nothing like where you originally started, and this takes your mind completely out of rhythm and action for what needs to be done.

To avoid distraction and increase productivity through staying in the moment, I suggest writing a daily list of priority tasks. This should be dictated by your sales goal, the amount of calls and prospecting messages you need to send based on your sales conversion and the amount of booked calls and meetings you need to attend to achieve that sales goal.

Focus could be described as "removing distraction". Get your tasks done and stay in line with your numbers. Remove anything that has you too focused on the future and not on the present actions that need to be taken today.

A tip to help you achieve this is when writing your priority list: ensure you start the day with the hardest tasks first. Once I started prioritising the hard work in my day, I became more productive and less anxious about those tasks in my business.

Stay in the moment and work your ass off. There is no avoiding it, and the future isn't promised.

ATTACHMENT

"I love working with my clients."

Is this something you say, or hope to say in the future? I can quite honestly say I do genuinely appreciate and enjoy working with all our agency clients and partners. It is my daily blessing to communicate and innovate new solutions for their customers and approach them in new ways.

But adoration and attachment are completely different beasts. If your business relationships are too emotionally fuelled, they can lead to heartache in a business setting that doesn't reward it.

Let me show you how dangerous attachment to your clients can be. Worse still, attachment to the revenue they bring to your business.

Let's say you sign a new client. They loved the strategy call and services you pitched and signed them up on, and they have paid upfront on the day for your $2000-plus fee. Now you start building their Facebook and Instagram ads and all of a sudden they are blown away by how solid your delivery for the campaign is. You follow the system and deliver the first draft of ads for their approval.

They give you a call and feedback that they are super excited about the campaign and you are good to launch.

You launch the campaign and now you have exceeded the cost-per-lead target for the client by more than 50 percent. They wanted leads at $20 per lead and you're generating leads for $10.

They get on a call and offer to take you out to lunch. You go to the meeting and have a great time. Laughter, jokes, stories about business, introductions and referrals to their network - it's all happening so fast! Exciting times, right?

You continue working on the campaign with the same energy and vigor you started with, but guess what? The results start tumbling down. Suddenly, you are creeping up to the minimum CPL required to achieve your target. Month two comes around and the bubble has burst. You're now generating leads at $40 each.

The phone starts ringing and it's your adored client. Some might assume at this point this person is your friend. But the tone isn't friendly. Things are not what they used to be. Although you appreciate and understand what the client is complaining about, how they are saying it makes you catch feels. They aren't extending the love they once did, and deep down you thought your relationship was because of who you were and not because of what you could do for them.

This has happened to more consultants that I've trained than I care to count. Deflated after riding the rollercoaster of friendship and collaboration when the results were hot, only to come back down to earth and feel heartbreak when business turns around. And then eventually the client leaves.

Here is another truth about this business I have come to learn over the past few years: you are a professional.

Professional and personal lives should not cross too often. Going for client meetings over lunch is a great way to become unproductive in the long term.

Every time you bask in the glory of your existing clients, you risk neglecting new clients you can help grow. If you need a pat on the back or recognition for your work, request it from your parents, partner, or a friend. I'm sure they will tell you how great you are upon request, and are less likely to leave if things go south.

Keep your professionalism intact at all times. Don't drink with clients. Don't talk too much about your personal life. Keep conversation in line with the reason you were brought together in the first place: to serve the needs of their customers through marketing.

If a client is adamant that you must socialise with them to do business together. treat that as a red flag.

As you grow your brand, the requests for coffee meet ups, lunches and dinners will increase. Try to understand the intentions behind such requests and ask if they serve the ultimate goals for your business and where you want to go.

In my own business, some of the best relationships and most valued members of my network are past or current clients. I attribute this to the emotional detachment I have towards them and the way in which we serve them. Whether they are buying from me or not, it is not a personal decision. They have their reasons for doing either.

My job is to simply offer solutions at an affordable price to the client. The decision to work together must come from them. If we do business and they leave that does not make them a bad person or poor businessperson. It simply means they have chosen what they feel is best for them. As a digital marketing consultant, you must respect those decisions with the same amount of respect you would like to receive from the marketplace.

I have had multiple clients commit deposits and recall them. This is common, and in the first year of business it can emotionally ruin you. You went through the entire process of gaining a payment and therefore commitment to the project only to have it ripped from underneath your feet. You built timelines and schedules, made draft ad copy and creative, maybe even started editing their existing content for ads, only to be told "the time isn't right," or "the funds are needed for something else". This can crush the weaker consultants in my program. But this is also what my mentorship program is built to do: guide you through this turmoil with simple truth.

Nothing is promised. Don't get attached.

Don't get into this business looking for love, friendship and deep meaningful social interactions. At the very best, these are by-products of delivering a world-class service to your clients. Do not mix up the professional service they are paying for with the personal emotions that come with achieving success.

You can have a digital agency with clients you enjoy serving and the occasional invitation to socialise and build a deeper connection outside of your billable hours. Both your time and your clients time is valuable. Do not waste it looking for excuses to play hopscotch and kiss-chase (metaphorically speaking, of course).

CHAPTER SIX

MAKE YOUR BUSINESS THE BEST IT CAN BE

If I told you that you were literally one call away from receiving up to $2000 into your business, how would you feel? Pretty excited, right?

If the prospect of $2000 isn't doing it for you, adjust that figure accordingly to what will significantly grow your business. In my experience, for most businesses in their first 365 days, $2000 per call is adequate.

Now put that into context. If you can close one client on a $2000 monthly retainer, you have just secured $24,000 of revenue for the year. If you close four clients in one month, you will be bringing $96,000 per year into your agency.

And that is what we are dealing with here. The reality that you are one call away from $2K. All of a sudden, success doesn't seem so far away, does it?

My first deal was a social media management offer with content creation included for only $500. It was a steal, and what really concerned me was that no one was buying it!

It was only after I took the plunge into being mentored that I began to understand how to price my services efficiently, based on the value we bring and not just the time we spend. The first deal for $5000 came two weeks after the beginning of my coaching. It was an event marketing client and I couldn't believe it. Finally, I had seen that with the right information and execution I could easily scale my business to over $10,000 per month, simply by repeating this process. And that is exactly what I did.

By the end of the second month after receiving paid guidance, I broke the $12,000 per month mark between four clients. This was when things began to get dramatically busy, and at times hectic. This chapter should serve as the foundation to your sales process, and by using these exact guidelines you can close your next $2000 to $4000. I have seen many consultants do it over and over again.

Please use and apply the above methods and send me an e-mail directly with your results at aaron@socialagendas.com. Our Black Ops Sales Script goes into much more detail and covers more scenarios you might encounter in your first sales calls. To get the most out of the script, you will need the full support service we give to all our mentees. If you are interested in learning more about pitching and closing deals, visit our Online Course Modules.

It is my pleasure to share this with you, because things would have moved a lot faster for me if I had known this at the beginning of my career.

You are already good enough to start selling. Now the question is: will you do the work?

The next section of this book will give you some practical tips on how to generate leads and make money in your first 365 days. It is not a substitute for joining our Agency Partner Program and getting access to the Black Ops Sales Script, but it is certainly a good place to start!

CHAPTER SEVEN

THE HUNT, THE CHASE, THE KILL

If you want to take actionable content away from this book, you are in the right place. "The chase, the hunt, the kill" is a metaphor for the approach you should have ingrained into your sales process (and your team's).

Each of these sections is about a different time period in the growth of your own company. Without a good understanding of sales alongside influence and persuasion you will forever be at the whim of those like myself who own the projects and deals that need to be fulfilled.

I personally own my deals. This means I dictate to my team how that work is done. I only have the opportunity to do this because I am proficient in recognising needs and delivering hyper-relevant solutions to prospects. This skill is transferable to all my clients' prospects too.

If you can get clear on how this works you will become a very highly valued member of the business world. You become the individual who is only one call away from closing a minimum of $1000 in any given business.

You can also own your deals, which will let you retain more of your profit margins when outsourcing the delivery of your campaigns.

I suggest that all agency owners I train should hire help after they hit the $6000 to $8000 per month mark. When delivery starts to become the focus of the business, it is time for you to get back on the tasks that are most difficult to outsource: sales.

PROSPECTING – THE HUNT

In this section I'm going to give you an easy and free method to begin generating inbound leads to pitch your services to. I'm going to tell you exactly what to say and how to get people into a position where they can consider the value that you bring to the table.

This strategy works on both platforms for generating leads as booked calls to give you the opportunity to sell. It will teach you exactly how to generate calls with high-value business owners in any niche using the social media platforms you already have.

Before launching this strategy, you will need an Instagram or similar social media profile. You will also need a calendar link set up for sending to prospects. The platform I recommend is youcanbook.me - you can use it to send prospects a link to book a call in your diary when the time is right.

The strategy is simple, and you can begin immediately. In the headline of your profile, write a specific job title that is relevant to the prospect. For example, this might be "Digital Marketing Consultant for Dental Practices". This is so when someone receives a message from you and reviews your profile, they know the exact nature of your business and potential benefits for them. This in turn gently qualifies them if you gain a response.

The sequence is built on a three-message script which will lead to a scheduled call link for them to book into your diary.

Step 1: Pick a certain niche you want to work with. This will change often so do not spend too long going back and forth on this.

Step 2: With that niche in mind search hashtags on Instagram to bring up content relevant to that niche. Search for #restaurants if your passion is to work in the dining niche.

Step 3: Look for relevant content and find the pages that are publishing it. Here are three things you will need to check to qualify a lead:

- Have they got more than 500 followers? If not, the profile could be fake and misleading.
- Are they posting frequently (at least once a month)? If not, the profile might not be active.
- Do you genuinely believe you can help their business?

If the answer to all three questions is "yes", you can move on to the next step.

Step 4: Once you find an ideal prospect, follow them and like three of their posts. Then contact them using the four-stage script below.

FIRST CONTACT SCRIPT

Stage 1: Complimentary/Introductory Stage

Open the conversation with a message complimenting the specific business and something that you can see they are doing on their profile.

<<Hi [prospect first name], I just wanted to say I love the work you are doing on [product/service/personal brand/project or something you like about the business].>>

<<Keep up the great work!>>

Stage 2: Rapport-Building Question

Only send this message after a response from the prospect.

In this section you will be asking a general question about the business itself.

<<How long have you been running the company? You seem very established.>>

After a response:

<<Amazing, how are you finding the journey so far?>>
OR

<<So [prospect name], what are you working on in your business currently? I would love to hear!>>

Stage 3: Ask the prospect another relevant question

<<How are you currently obtaining leads? Take me through the good, the bad and the ugly of each method!>>

Stage 4: Seal the Deal and Close on a Booked Call

In this stage you will offer to get on a call with the prospect.

<<I don't usually do this, but I love your hustle and mindset [insert prospect name]. Let's hop on a one-to-one call as I know some ways I can be of value to you on your journey!>>

<<[insert scheduler link e.g. www.youcanbook.me/yourcompanyname]>>

Once you have sent the scheduler link you must follow up. If they book in immediately, tell them how excited you are for the call. If they do not book in immediately, they may want more context on what the call shall be about.

If they ask for more information, reply:

<<On the call I'd love to share a few things that could increase your [relevant outcome]! After hearing about what you're doing currently I'm very confident it will help.>>

<<Did the link above work ok?>>

When repeated enough times, this prospecting technique will become habit. You will become addicted to the sequence and, more importantly, the power of it when you start to see the calls coming through.

If you are using a personal profile it is important to start framing your content in a way that will show the prospect you are professional and serious about your business. Avoid posting political or polarising content.

View your social media profile as a place to generate opportunities to grow your business. In the next chapter we will talk about how to start positioning your content around the result you desire.

You have now started to generate booked calls. People are genuinely interested in how you can help their business and have an idea about who you are and what you do. Pretty exciting stuff, right?

PITCHING - THE CHASE

Now it is time for you to pitch. You know how to generate calls. Before telling you about what to say, how to say it and when to say it, there are some key points I want you to have deeply ingrained in your mind. The call is simply a meeting that occurs without the need to physically see your prospect face-to-face. This means you can work with overseas businesses, and you can be flexible about where you work and take calls from. I want you to think of your calls process in three stages: pre-call, during the call, and post-call. For now, let's focus on the pre-call preparation. Before any call, I want you to be prepared to give yourself the best chance for success.

PRE-CALL

REMOVE DISTRACTIONS

Depending on where you are taking the call from, the amount of distractions that you need to remove will vary. You need a quiet environment whether that is indoors or outdoors. I have closed some of my biggest deals while pacing up and down my garden, and even a couple sitting on the loo. Anything goes in the first year, but I've got my act together since and this isn't something I would promote.

If you are taking calls from an environment that isn't an office you will need to remove distractions such as other people, televisions and loud noises. Even your lunch sitting on the table can be a distraction. Do not allow anything to distract you from the task at hand.

HANDS-FREE KIT

This can be wired or wireless and will fast become an essential tool to your performance. As well as being more comfortable than holding your phone up to your ear for up to 30 minutes at a time, the handsfree kit lets you open up your body language, which comes through on the call. This freedom of movement lets you switch from active listening to writing notes, and even to having the seamless ability prompt yourself with your sales script if you have one. Your sales pitch is a performance, having the physical freedom to react and respond to the call is one key ingredient that will contribute to your success.

NOTEPAD

The old trusted notepad. Your secret weapon. If you don't have one, get one. It is more powerful than you realise during a sales call. What type of information should you be writing in this? Everything. Bullet points. Short sharp pieces of vital information you are learning from your prospect while deeply qualifying their needs.

I have personally gone blank during a call many times, and the notebook is the cure. You're vibing with the prospect, flowing freely with your trusted hands-free kit plugged into your ears. Everything is groovy, you're in your zone. Then it comes to the offer and close phase of the call and you can't remember the specific outcomes the prospect told you they want solved. Uh-oh. Then, you look down at your notes and BOOM! You're back in the game.

A sales or strategy call should create the opportunity to present a prospect with a hyper-relevant offer that solves their current problem. Without the specific numbers and the right information collected and gathered through a call, this will become much more difficult. Don't make anything harder than it needs to be. Have your notes ready to be deployed. This will show your prospect you are organised, and that you care to learn about their needs on a deeper level.

PREPARE YOUR BODY LANGUAGE

In my experience you can tap into a lot more energy standing up on a sales call than sitting down. If you cannot stand, you can still apply these principles of body language and expressing yourself freely by holding your shoulders back and head up.

It comes back to energy. Ideas come to me quickest when I am in flow with the energy around me. being in motion often kickstarts my brain into motion. When on a sales call you are constantly leading and pacing vocally.

I want you to think of this concept as if you are a military trainer with a new cadet. This cadet knows they should be running at your pace. But simply knowing they should do something is not enough to overcome the current pain they are enduring to keep up. The best form of action for you as the trainer is to pace and lead.

When leading, you direct the prospect's attention to where they want to be. This is usually a greater volume of sales and revenue, or a more efficient sales process. When pacing, you come back to their current position and empathise with the pain of their current challenges in their business to achieve their goals. As the expert that knows how to get them to their desired destination, standing up during the sales call process lets you summon more energy to lead the call. This should result in more confidence, free flowing ideas and easier objection handling, as well as more tailored and specific solutions for your prospect.

You are now prepared for the call and you're ready to hit that dial button. During the call there are five main areas I want you to focus on.

FIVE STEPS TO A SOLID SALES CALL

Step 1: Achieve Instant Familiarity

Even when attending a booked call appointment, you cannot assume that the prospect will remember who you are and what the call might be about. If you hop on and they are unfamiliar with who you are the first thing to remember is that is fine.

There is no need to get emotional about it. To achieve instant familiarity, you need to know the prospect's name. When they book in a call using your youcanbook. me schedule link, they will have to fill the name field.

One way to achieve instant familiarity is through the following phrases:

"[Prospect Name], how's your day going?"
OR:
"[Prospect Name], how's your week been so far?"
Wait for response.
"Amazing, what are you working on right now?"

The whole purpose of this is to make the prospect think "Do I know this person?"

As they are figuring it out, their natural response is to reply. Say this opening line with joy and high energy. Imagine it as seeing an old friend for the first time in years.

Once you have completed some initial back-and-forth, they should have caught up to who you are. If they can't remember and you can tell they are too polite to ask, tell them who you are without having to spell it out.

"First of all, I want to thank you for taking the time to book in the call after our brief conversation on Instagram."

Step 2: Frame the Reason for the Call

This will help them understand why they are here. Without framing the call, it will be hard for the prospect to justify giving you their time if they are busy running their business or marketing department. Use the following phrase:

(Excited Tone) "I'm really excited to be on this call with you. I have got so much I want to speak to you about, but before all of that, what is it that you want to gain from this call, [prospect name]?"

This simple yet very effective positioning of the call lets your prospect start discussing their needs from the get-go. If you got the booked call via the organic prospecting method using Instagram, you might be concerned that they will say they booked in the call at your request, but most people will not remember the booking was made under your influence.

Instead, they will most likely begin discussing potential solutions you can provide to problems that they are facing with their online marketing.

You need to understand what they want to gain from the call. This could be how you work, past results you've achieved, pricing of your services, or even why you invited them to come onto the call. You can then start to deliver relevant information on your skillset, how you can help them and, most importantly, how much it costs.

But before you close, you will need a solid qualification process. I am excited to share more information with you about the Black Ops Sales Script we have developed in our online course, but before that, Step 3 is extremely important to understand. Are you ready to jump in?

Step 3: Ask High-Quality Questions

The person asking the questions is the person leading the conversation. When you ask a question, you already know the types of responses you might get, which allow you to shift the dialogue in a specific direction. For you as a consultant, the backbone of your qualifying call is sensitive information. The current results of the businesses activities and the target results the business would like to achieve.

What are some high-quality questions to ask a business owner?

"So, talk to me [Prospect Name], how are you getting on with your Marketing/Lead Generation/Advertising right now?"

Feed off the information they give you and slow down.

"What are you working towards: what are you trying to achieve? What is your target monthly revenue?"

Response.

"Ok, and how close are you to that currently?"

Response.

"Have you ever worked with somebody for *Social Media Marketing/Facebook Ads/Marketing Funnels before?"

Step 4: Qualify their Answers

Something important to remember throughout your sales call process is that although the call might be going fantastically well, the prospect still might not trust you with sensitive information. You must empathise with this and respond by qualifying their answers specifically. Sometimes instead of withholding information, they will deceive you with false numbers, overstating sales or the success of the business due to ego or insecurities.

Qualifying their answers will help your intuition sieve out the truth from the lies. This is important to maintain accuracy in your sales process.

In my first year of agency life I was gullible to prospects and their false representations of their business. This led to wasted time on proposals and pitches that, truth be told, I wish I had never sent.

There is no specific phrasing to use, because the answers you are qualifying will vary. A good rule of thumb is after receiving the answer to a high-quality question, ask another question in relation to their answer and gauge their response. This might look like:

"How close are you to your target monthly revenue per month?"

Response: "We are achieving it currently bringing in revenue at around $90,000 per month."

"Amazing, and what price point is your top-selling product in the business?"

Response: "Our top product is currently the Dyson Vacuum cleaner that sells at $250."

"Ok and as a percentage what portion of your total monthly revenue is attributed to the Dyson Vacuum?"
Response: "Probably around 80 percent."

At this point following the previous sales call tips you will have written all these numbers in your notebook. You might then want to do a quick calculation:

Revenue x Percentage of Dyson sales = Revenue from Dyson sales
$90,000 x 0.8 = $72,000
and

Revenue from Dyson sales / Dyson price point = Units of Dyson sold per month
$72,000 / 250 = 288 units per month

Now that you have an idea of what sales should approximately be attributed to Dyson sales in units you may want to ask the prospect:

"Approximately how many units of Dyson Vacuum are you selling per month?"

If the answer the prospect gives you is nowhere near the 288 units you have calculated, this should be an indication that either you have got something wrong or the prospect has.

This could be unintentional or intentional. Regardless of the reason behind it, you must qualify your prospect's answers in such depth that everything makes logical sense. If you don't have accurate targets and figures the entire pitch could be a waste of time.

Step 5: Practice Active Listening with Affirmations

Active listening is simple. This is the art of listening without the intention to reply. Do you listen to your people, prospects and clients during conversation, or simply wait for your turn to speak? The danger of not actively listening is that you might miss vital pieces of information that you need to address.

In the sales call, address every single word your prospect says. If they ask a question, don't ignore it. If they describe struggle or frustration with their current marketing process, empathise with that. Don't be too scripted.

The Black Ops Sales Script we have created for mentee consultants has cleared over $1.5 million since its inception. That is both for agencies and clients' products that we help sell over calls on their behalf. The five principles we have discussed are the backbone to this process.

You might have noticed that all the factors in a solid sales call come back to one core characteristic a successful agency owner must have: caring. You have to care to help the people you work with. You must genuinely want to serve them so brilliantly that they are blown away by your professionalism, skill and execution. Don't be amateur. There are enough people doing that already. Use the five steps to a solid sales call to be sharp, authoritative and understanding.

Being a good business person should simply be an extension of who you already are. If you are a greed-driven egomaniac only interested in serving your own interests, please stop reading and use none of my advice. On the other hand, if you are genuinely someone interested in being rewarded for the results and work you deliver to other businesses please continue to learn from my experience in your first 365.

CLOSING ON YOUR OFFER – THE KILL

It's game time!

You have gone from being a complete stranger to getting a booked call, to qualifying your prospect in one conversation. Now you are ready to present and close on your offer. Everything you have done has led you to this point. Get excited, but remain composed. Your sales process is a numbers game based on your lifestyle calculation: how much you need to earn to live the lifestyle of your dreams. Don't focus on the value of the money; rather focus on the impact that it can have on your life and those you care for around you. The more you make, the more you can give.

Before asking for a transaction, you must present a hyper-relevant offer. Your entire sales process fails without a clear solution for your prospect's problem. This purchasing decision should make sense to your prospect, both logically and emotionally.

I recommend and teach having a minimum of five core service offers in your agency that differ in delivery based on what phase your client's business is in. These could include strategy and consultation calls; full Facebook and Instagram ads build; launch and management; content creation; reports; landing pages; email marketing; messenger marketing bots; the list goes on.

Currently in my own agency we have over 15 core offers which escalate in price and value depending on who we are working with. If you have no idea what your offers are, here is a quick rundown of what you can easily learn to deliver through the right training and mentorship.

Offer 1: Consultation Call (2 Hour) $297 - $497

With knowledge of social media marketing you can assess and give consultation on a company's social media presence and effectiveness based on their activity compared to their competitors. But this is not the sole purpose of the call.

The consultation call works nicely to debate and consider different strategies they should consider. The next offer should be a natural discussion and progression. Through this consultation call you have framed the "what" of how they should proceed and Offer 2 is based on "how" you can help them achieve the goals and targets set out in this call.

Offer 2: Done for You Facebook and Instagram Advertising Service (1 Month) $1497 - $2497

This offer is to deliver the build, launch and maintenance of Facebook and Instagram advertising campaigns for one entire month. This includes design of ads.

Offer 3: Offer 2 + Content Creation ($1997 - $2997)

This offer includes everything to run their Facebook and Instagram campaigns for one month alongside shooting a content creation day with the business or client you are pitching. This is best accomplished by hiring a videographer or content creator for the day.

Adding a content day would be relevant if your client has no creative content to distribute through your Facebook ads. Understanding what content they have already produced comes from asking high quality questions.

Now you have some offers to pitch. If you have zero skills in any of the service offerings you should consider investing in a course or mentor who you can see is actively practising this in the marketplace. It goes without saying that our programs work, as you already know from the number of consultants we have helped on their journey.

When it comes to closing, your job is to present your offer alongside the result you are trying to achieve.

Here is one way of phrasing this, assuming you have the information from the qualification questions above:

"So if we could help get you to [target revenue per month] within the next four weeks, how would you feel?

Wait for response.

"Great, so I'm really excited to tell you about [offer name], shall I walk you through how it works?"

The question above is about gaining something I call "permission to sell". This is consent from your prospect to proceed into discussing the product and how it works and can help solve their solution. This appeals to the logical part of their brain.

The first question, related to feeling, is to appeal to the emotions of your prospect. It allows you to frame the future and allows them to experience how they might feel once their targets are achieved.

After describing and ensuring the prospect understands your service, you need to agree on relevancy.

"Does that sort of make sense [prospect name]?"

Response or affirmation.

"Now that you know how it works, how relevant does [offer name] sound for helping your business grow?"

Wait for a positive response to relevance.

"Amazing. So I'm sure you're aware there is an investment involved, right?"

Response.

"Good, so the cost of getting started with our [offer name] is just [offer price]."

If the response from the prospect is positive, ask:

"Great, so how would you like to make that payment?"

If the response is tentative, diffuse the situation:

"Ok that's fine."

Your job as a closer begins after the offer has been presented. The only way you will present an offer to a client is if they have qualified themselves and given you permission to sell.

If they do not progress, do not continue with the call.

They are not ready for an offer if they have disqualified themselves as an ideal prospect.

If they are ready to go through with the transaction, be ready with a Paypal.me link or similar payment method ready to send to them while you are still on the call. PayPal takes a cut, but this is a quick and easy payment process that gives the client some comfort. You can also set up PayPal invoices, but at this point speed is key. Now they are ready to move forward, your job is to make collecting payment as easy as possible.

In the Black Ops Sales Script, we have created many options for handling objections to getting started. Here is a taster with a couple of these methods to conquer the money objection, which is by far the most common pushback from clients.

OBJECTION HANDLING

Money Objection: If you receive an objection about the cost or price, your immediate response must be to diffuse and qualify their objection.

"Ok, that's fine. Is it an affordability issue right now, or that you don't understand the value the campaign will bring to your business yet?"

Depending on the answer to this question, you will have a clear picture on how to proceed. If it is an affordability issue you can discuss options for payment based on their affordability. For example:

"Awesome. I don't want affordability to be an issue for you [prospect name], so tell me, how close can you get to [offer price] today?"

If the issue is that they aren't comfortable pulling the trigger because of understanding or confidence in your ability to deliver the results. You must go back to the section before the offer and focus on how it works. You might have missed the opportunity to address their burning concern or objection to working with you earlier in the call. You might have been rushing to the offer and overlooking their original needs.

You can also go back to the education section and expand on who you are, what you do, and why you do it. As much as it is about the what and the how of your services, it is also about the who. You are responsible for inserting the appropriate amount of your story and business journey.

For example, this works well by empathising and linking their pain towards online marketing to your own journey when you were an absolute newbie:

"I understand where you're coming from. I remember when I first started using Facebook Advertising and didn't have the right strategy or information to get results on the platform too."

"It was only once I began working with the right information and people that I was able to achieve results, which is sort of the position you're in right now."

Phrases like the above will allow you to bring your own experience into the conversation without being specific, especially if you are a new marketer and they are your first ever prospect.

It seems ridiculous, but let me assure you, equipped with the above language and principles I have seen countless mentees close deals within their first week of actively looking for them.

CHAPTER EIGHT

POSITIONING AND PERSONAL BRANDING

Can you close deals without positioning? Of course. Will closing deals be easier with good positioning? Of course!

Business is based on trust. You have to give it to receive it. When you are prospecting you extend trust: you are saying you believe the prospect is who they say they are and their products should be promoted.

And trust goes both ways. When a business evaluates whether you are trustworthy enough to deliver them the results they want, you can't afford to have leaks in your personal brand.

Nobody wants to be your first. It is simply too much risk. If we lived in a fair society people would give equal opportunity, but we don't, and no one cares about your feelings. Clients just want more sales.

When building your personal brand, you need to start projecting who you are onto the world, accompanied by your belief systems. This will build the basis of your content, and when you have a certain amount of that content in circulation people will start paying more attention.

When you have their attention you can begin converting that into sales opportunities and growing your business. Here are three pillars of personal branding that will give you practical guidance:

MY STORY: BRANDING DAY

When talking about building a personal brand there are some key elements to consider, but the easiest way I've found to simplify this process is using something a prospect said to me in my first year.

It was a catering company specialising in events. The prospect asked me about the previous results I had got for clients. Not really knowing what I was doing, I began reeling off everything I had ever done for anyone in business and alike. I barely refrained from telling them about the cups of tea I had successfully delivered to my mother over the years.

Jokes aside, the prospect simply replied;

"Aaron, I really like you, and think we could probably work together, but don't tell me. Show me."

That quote has stuck with me ever since. After receiving this information, I quickly realised it was not enough to simply have a client on a call.

I started to consider how much information I could give about who I am and what I've done without having to force feed it down their throats on the first call. That was the birth of my focus on personal branding.

I went to Argos and bought a Nikon D5300 Camera using my Argos credit card. I immediately handed it to my partner, put on a suit and began my first ever personal branding day.

My company has now delivered over 300 personal branding shoots over the past four years. It is a cornerstone for many of the authority-driven brands we work with. This is not to be confused with our content creation offer that is more focused on product and "social first" content production.

What was the result of that personal branding day, and why is it a part of the six-month agency partner program I have created? When you are starting out, the biggest thing that you are missing is credibility.

CONTENT

"Content is King and distribution is Queen."

Having a good content strategy is simple when you understand why you are doing it. As a digital consultant, your social media profiles and accounts must be focused and centred around you because you are the one who will be sending people offers in the first year of your agency.

To give you some inspiration for your content strategy with clients, we have several "content pillars" that we build from.

EDUCATION:

Educational content is exactly what it says on the tin. Use your knowledge of a particular subject to position yourself as an expert. This could be something extremely simple to you, but to your non-marketing-savvy business-owner audience, your subject matter might be something completely out of their depth.

Educational content could involve you facing a camera and speaking about a certain topic, or you sharing a screen and overdubbing the video using a software such as Loom.

You may want to start by educating people on the different services you offer. After that, you might begin educating on the different results you have delivered for clients.

You can also discuss software, technology and apps that you use in your workflow. The list goes on, but the important thing to remember about this content pillar is the subject you are speaking about is less important than the credibility you build when speaking about it.

INSPIRATION:

This is based upon your story: where you have been, where you are and where you are going. This digital agency life is a journey where you will meet many others on a similar path to you. The inspirational content is to serve as a virtual landscape on which you can meet people to do business. Consider it a platform being extended between you and the people you wish to speak to.

Inspirational content can come in many forms, and I recommend opening up about your thoughts on a variety of subjects. People aren't as interested in marketing as you might like them to be. That is an opportunity. That is why we exist.

Opening up about your thoughts involves putting yourself out there and being vulnerable. People will be drawn to you because of this, and will begin to build trust and feel comfortable sharing sensitive information with you. They are simply reciprocating what you have already done for them. If you need inspiration you can easily see this type of approach in practice if you go to my Instagram account @aaron_branch - pay particular attention to the captions below each post.

Now it's your turn! Share your story to the world.

ENTERTAINMENT:
Entertaining content can be anything around yourself, your brand, bloopers, or anything else that grabs attention. In my profile, I try to introduce humour. Business is not the stiff corporate world that it used to be. Use entertaining content such as vlogs, Instagram stories and live video streams to give people a much closer, less post-produced image of yourself and your business.

Show your viewers other interests in your life that aren't necessarily related to your digital agency, but are related to who you are and your passions. For me of course this is sport, basketball. I am not shy about sharing this part of my life and it is one area that I champion to entertain and also to show that I am human!

This content pillar can become very easy to fulfil when you get into a rhythm. But please don't share everything in your life. Remember your prospects will see this content. You must produce content with the audience in mind.

PLATFORMS

Facebook, Instagram, LinkedIn and YouTube are currently the best social media platforms to focus on. Understanding the advantages of each is essential for your growth. Facebook and Instagram are where you will do most of your prospecting, which means having good activity and consistent uploads is essential on these platforms. LinkedIn is a bit trickier to get traction on early in your first 365 days, depending on the strength of your profile. Once you have a profile set up, you can target different niches and individuals with influence very quickly. YouTube is the platform to build out as much social proof as possible, and is brilliant for indexing you on Google for when someone types your name into a search.

This is important, because if a prospect isn't sure about working with you, they might turn to Google first. If you have relevant and educational content on the subject you want to help them with such as Facebook ads, it will help the prospect feel more settled about your skill set and authority on the subject of marketing, even if your videos don't have a lot of likes and comments.

SOCIAL PROOF

All your content is designed to build social proof. This means that when you interrupt a prospect's day, they can easily check you out on multiple platforms and see you are worth their time. They can clearly see you are focused on your craft and that you also have more to show about yourself than just your digital marketing expertise.

This content can become the launch pad of your digital strategy. It is essential for fast-tracking your progress in a competitive market. It takes an investment of time and money to produce content, but you should not underestimate the power of your existing technology. Do you have a phone that can shoot decent quality videos? If so, you are good to go.

If you don't have video editing software on your laptop or the skills to edit them, you can use simple and free phone apps such as Inshot. This app will help you achieve amazing results very quickly when it comes to post-producing both video and images.

When distributing your content, aim for consistency and volume over quality. Remember that you are producing content for positioning, social proof and attention that you can convert into opportunities. Do not get hung up on the vanity metrics of likes, shares, followers or subscribers. Consider your digital marketing profiles as a finely tuned engine for producing leads and sales for your business.

CHAPTER NINE

GIVE YOURSELF THE BEST OPPORTUNITY TO SUCCEED

AGENCY PARTNER PROGRAM

I would be doing you a disservice by not talking about the one thing that has changed more lives than any of my other work. Through my digital agency we have cleared beyond seven figures, and it fills me with pride to say we have achieved that. But in some ways, I feel the same today as I did more than four years ago when I started.

I still have an aching amount of unfulfilled potential within me, and that is what keeps driving me forwards. But there is a big difference between the life I once knew and the life I have today. Aside from finances, the information, systems and processes that I am operating on make everything easier. They are simply better and more advanced. In saying that, I know it would have compromised my growth if I had received these systems too soon.

As my agency grew, I began to get requests to learn how I did it. After giving advice away, people still needed more advice, which has led me to building a mentorship program. This program systematically serves the immediate needs of beginner and advanced digital agency owners based on their business income achieved.

If you want to learn more about the program or sign on to be a mentee, contact me directly on aaron@socialagendas.com.

EVERYTHING I WISH I HAD

When I started my digital marketing journey, I endured serious doubts and isolation from what felt like the entire world. I did not have any peers who could understand and empathise with what I was going through.

Not having that support system was one of the most difficult parts about starting out. Knowing that I was "winging it" didn't give me the absolute confidence I needed to close the types of deals I wanted to be a part of.

It was only when I invested in myself and found a mentor that the pieces of the puzzle started to come together. I gained a clear, systemic approach for closing and delivering the services that clients' businesses actually need.

After that initial investment I made on a credit card, I closed my first $5000 deal for an event marketing service which included Facebook ads, content creation, landing pages and event sales support for an additional commission.

It was mind-blowing to see the immediate impact of the new information I was operating on. It then led me to look at investing further into my own education online. After doing some research I was really disappointed at the standard of courses that were on offer. There were many pitching Facebook ads skills but very few showing the exact formula for actually signing a deal from start to finish and all the other aspects of growing an agency.

I also didn't like that almost all the programs lacked any real personal touch. They were straight buy-online-see-you-next-time deals. After studying the people behind the courses, I realised quickly that they weren't actually operating successful agencies at all. Their entire business was based around being educators, which for me meant they might be out of touch with current practises. I wanted to feel valued and a part of a community in which I could grow my skills while sharing my journey with like-minded people.

I wanted resources that were actively in use that I could easily duplicate and model. Instead all I kept seeing was "millionaire mindset" and "quit your 9-5". It was becoming frustrating. I vowed that when I reached a certain level of success I would give back and allow others to do the same.

This birthed two different programs under the Agency Partner Program. The One Month Mentorship for those working towards their first $8000 per month and the Six Month Mentorship for those looking to scale past the $10,000 per month mark. After launching these programs, the demand soared and I'm happy to say that today, through a rigorous qualification process, I have personally trained and mentored over 200 consultants.

HOW CAN IT SERVE YOU?

The target for the One Month Mentorship is to get you earning your next $2000 $4000 within four weeks. This is through a step-by-step process starting with establishing your goals and target income based on your actual lifestyle and interests. We couple this with a personality test to find strengths and weaknesses that might hinder or aid you during your agency's development. Once we have the estimated expenses for the lifestyle you want, we add an additional 30 percent to that figure for savings and investments.

We then break your target income down into actual sales per month based on five products and offers that you can quickly plug and play into your agency. These offers differ in pricing and value, but can easily be delivered with the training in the program.

The program is all about client acquisition and delivery of services. It includes all the resources I wish I had when going after that first $4000 benchmark in my agency.

Sales is - and should remain - a huge focus for you, but it is useless selling a service that you do not know how to deliver. This training is designed to give you those skills and core competencies in an easy-to-digest way that can give you confidence and competency to run a four-figure agency within a month of starting.

If you are interested in taking your agency to the next level visit https://www.agencypartnerprogram.training

THE DECISION

Your life is the result of all the actions you did and did not take. Action is the key ingredient for any growth. Doing nothing will get you nothing. This book and the information within it have the ability to drastically change your circumstances when applied with the right effort and energy. There are literally thousands of businesses out there waiting to hear from you and work with you at this very second. The question really becomes: are you willing to put in the work to find and help them?

If you are ready to act, I would love to hear about your approach and the results you have got after reading this book. Please don't be a stranger; take advantage of reaching out to me through social media or through my email address: aaron@socialagendas.com.

Make the decision today to go out and deliver huge amounts of value into the marketplace and I guarantee you that everything you have ever wanted and desired will naturally follow.

CHAPTER TEN

MY FIRST 365: THE BENTLEY CLIENT

Let me finish off this book with a funny story from my first year in business.

I had been pursuing a prospect for at least 5 weeks and had previously pitched them a social media management retainer. This was before I knew about the power of Facebook ads and how rapidly they could have an impact. With my new knowledge I reached out to the prospect again telling them I had got it wrong the first time and what they actually needed were services which originally I hadn't thought were relevant to them.

This prospect was a wealthy individual and someone I would come to learn a lot about business from. I did not know at the time that this was the beginning of something huge. After my second pitch for a meeting over the call (I hadn't yet mastered closing over the phone), I managed to secure a face-to-face meeting.

They were busy, and insisted the only time they could take this meeting would be while they were having vehicle repairs done in Birmingham. The vehicle was a Bentley Continental GT, and was being repaired at a Lamborghini Dealership.

The meeting was over 40 minutes' drive from where I was, and I would have to arrive in my blue Peugeot 206. Calling it a rust bucket would be a compliment. How was I supposed to walk into that meeting with authority if I was pulling up to the meeting in that? I was panicking and wondering whether to turn the meeting down.

I was having somewhat of an anxiety attack, but fortunately I came to my senses and got in the car. There I was in a full suit with a printed proposal pitching the biggest deal I had ever pitched in my career, pulling up in a car that looked worth less than my watch. I pulled up to the dealership sticking out like a sore thumb among the striking colours of the Lamborghinis around me.

My car's central locking was manual, so I had to place the key in the door to lock and unlock. The seconds it took to get that done felt like hours.

I did not have enough time to prepare a way to avoid putting my Peugeot in plain sight. Thank goodness the client was inside the building when I arrived.

Sweating and full of anticipation I greeted the client and pitched them advertising services in the region of $3000. They enjoyed my pitch and partially accepted my proposal. I was elated, but then something terrible happened.

Their car was ready. My heart sank. There wasn't enough time to get out before them and there was no Plan B to hide my car. There I was telling the owner of the business how much money we were going to make together, meanwhile I was driving around in $400 worth of wheels and engine. In terms of authority and positioning, it was a suicide mission. I couldn't even stay behind in the building because we were in the Lamborghini private lounge for customers only.

Keeping my composure, I opened the front door and we exited the building. The client started scouting the car park to see which vehicle might be mine. What vehicle I had assigned to my brand. And then it happened.

We shook hands and said goodbye. I began my slow descent towards the vehicles. I could feel the eyes piercing through the back of my head. At this moment I had to own it. I got my keys out and went straight to the door. Opened it up, jumped in and shamefully drove away. I never even looked back. I felt like a mug. It wasn't the damage to my ego that was bothering me but the damage to the opportunity I may have just compromised.

The following day all I could think about was the meeting and the verbal commitment they had given me. I was waiting for the right moment to follow up. I tried to hold off, but the urges were too much. There was too much riding on it. I was bouncing off the walls.

I plucked up the courage and try to call. Unscheduled. First mistake. They didn't answer, and I didn't leave a voicemail. Second mistake.

I went back to the drawing board. I crafted a well-written email to follow up and clicked send around two hours later. Still no reply.

I fell back into my insecurities about what they must think of me. The nerve, the audacity. They owned a Bentley; cars meant the world to them. They represented success in the prospect's world. I heard nothing back.

Until the next day. My shallow assumptions were wrong. They didn't even mention it once. They couldn't care less as far as I could tell, and I managed to sign the deal and received payment in full the following day.

The moral of this story is to go into every environment as you perceive yourself to be, even with the incredibly huge contradictions that often follow you around when starting out in your business life.

Embrace the beginning, and these uncomfortable occurrences that are sometimes unavoidable. I can assure you the things you think other people care about the most are often not what they are focused on. We went on to bill this client over six figures in fees and enjoyed a very healthy relationship during the course of our work together.

Don't let anything be an excuse to your progression. We all start from somewhere. No entrepreneur was born with a digital marketing funnel in their hands. Your focus should be simply to begin and improve.

Good luck.

TESTIMONIALS

Aaron is an absolute character to be around. He is such an inspiration and you can really feel the energy when you are in the room with him. This man has changed my life more than anyone will ever know. When I say there isn't a human being like him I really mean that! Thank you for everything my man. I'm forever grateful.

Luke Greeny, Miller Digital Marketing Agency

I've had the pleasure of knowing Aaron since he was 14 years young.

He got on a train after school, then walked a mile to the gym. His devotion and hard work was incredible and his skill set in 2 years was incredible.

It is no surprise to me that Aaron is so successful in everything he does. He is dedicated, loyal, talented and incredibly hard working and this makes him the born leader that he is.

A massive role model within business and sport.

Matt Coles, Spartans Basketball Club

In an age of gurus, clowns, and charlatans, Aaron Branch stands both literally and figuratively high above all the nonsense in the social media marketing space. Still more impressive is the fact that these foundations run so deep whilst staying at the forefront of the field replicating his results for others.

I first met Aaron at a free event he had put on in Kensington called Millennial Marketing Mastery back in 2019. I had no intention of buying anything that day but ended the day having signed up to a month of mentorship with him because I knew I had to partner with him. Let this illustrate Aaron's ability to sell solely with the value of his digital marketing expertise and pragmatic no-fluff approach to get results fast.

I now consider myself part of the family that Aaron has built at Social Agendas. Something anyone who works with him will instantly feel due to his infectious energy, authenticity, and sincerity in helping others to grow.

Curtis Douglas, Acorn Pie Digital Marketing Agency

Aaron Branch is the guy that is a team player and always looking to expand his team. He will help you progress in any field, he will bring you along and push you to your potential. For me and anyone knowing Aaron or worked with him he's a barrel of laughs, he looks after you and its always progres-

sion over perfection! Top Mentor. Thanks Aaron. Keep doing what you are doing brother.

Kyle Preston, Preston Visuals

One thing I can say about Aaron and his team (specifically Jack) is that they really are here to support you and give you the help that you need, especially when they see that you're genuinely trying. For that I am forever grateful.

I first came across Social Agendas about a month after I was introduced to the Social Media Marketing world and frankly, I was quite lost and didn't know where to start. I had a lot of doubt in my abilities and on the coaching day Aaron really made me realise that I just had to go out there and do it! That was the only way to get started. This confidence that I gained in knowing that Aaron and Jack were there to support me once I did my part is what really changed things for me. Even to this day, they have made it very clear to me that their doors are always open.

Thank you both for everything!

Hawa

Aaron often reminds me of myself when it comes to business, he is passionate and relentless when it comes to doing what he loves and this is originally how we started to work together, through his pursuit in making sure I give FB Ads a try. Having helped my business in the first 6 weeks make over 5 figures a month it showed me the importance of social media and how it can have a huge impact on the growth of your business. My advice is you'll gain a lot more then you could lose, you're in good hands with Aaron Branch!

Daniel Pollard, CEO Repwear Fitness

Came across Aaron's page via his own ad through Instagram. I already had goals this year to boost my market through digital marketing. It was like fate I had found him. I took a month to watch his page closely and analysed who his worked with and working with and how they are doing now. The last point that helped me pick him is his association with Birminghams Chambers of commerce.

Carrying out my bespoke training package with him allowed me to learn new tricks and boost my confidence in investing in budgets I would not have invested in before. With Aaron's expertise I was comfortable to take his lead, trust him and see what comes from it. The result was phenomenal. We hit our record breaking footfall at our monthly Muslim Market of up to 700 shoppers! His been a pleasure to work with and with the knowledge learnt it has taken so much stress of myself. He is really easy going and totally worth the investment! If you want to boost your business. Aaron is your man!

Yasmin, MD and Events Organiser @m_instashop Birminghams Monthly Muslim Market

Mr Aaron Branch, the man who saved my life.

[His] Mentorship completely opened my whole mindset about the whole online business industry as I was completely oblivious to this prior from only having experience from working at Subway and in a call centre. Unarguably the best investment I've made in my life as it's paved way to build my network and seek new opportunities.

Husnain Suhail

I've used a lot of agencies in the past who promise the world but upon using them clearly show their lack of knowledge around marketing funnels and measuring campaigns. I grew tired of this until I met Aaron at social agendas. My first conversation with Aaron gave me full confidence that he knew how marketing funnels work, and his experience and results from previous clients spoke for itself. Right away our values aligned and we connected and shortly after Aaron started working with us who very quickly boosted our marketing to the next level. We ran monthly events that were always sold out! On top of this, he grew our brand with growing exposure. What I love about Aaron is that you get bags of energy and he totally gets the ambition and message. It's not about the money, it's about the message and serving a purpose, which naturally brings in the rewards and Aaron totally gets that.

Kenny Sahota, Amilli Property Group

Aaron Branch is a leading force within the social media industry. Aaron's dedication to his craft coupled with his humility to open doors for people around him ensure that Aaron carry's the baton for our generation. Knowing that I have in my corner fills me with confidence that I can reach all of my business goals and overcome any obstacle. Aaron, thank you for equipping me with the tools to succeed.

John Shepherd, Shepherd Social

Aaron has spent years successfully starting and scaling businesses and is one of the most energetic, impressive and passionate people I have ever met. Over the past number of years of knowing him, I continue to be blown away by his tenacity of purpose and his trail-blazing attitude towards the projects that he works on.

Aran Spencer-Higgins, Managing Director, Social Buff

I met Aaron a month after starting my own agency, I didn't really have any direction in terms of who I wanted to work with and how I wanted to operate as an agency.

Having signed up to the mentorship with Aaron we quickly identified key areas where I lacked knowledge and areas that required improvement. It opened me eyes to the work required to build a successful agency.

Aaron's years of experience meant I didn't need to make the mistakes that he'd made but more importantly he had the vision to see what path I was on and knew that with the accountability and support the opportunities for growth within my agency and personally were limitless.

I know I would't be in the position I am today, with the agency I've built and continue to build if it wasn't for Aaron. He continues to be great mentor but also a great friend.

Thank You!
Oliver Blackhurst, Hamilton Media

I've worked with Aaron and his team on a few occasions now, firstly on a Facebook Ads training course. The amount it taught me certainly managed to take my business to the next level. After this, I decided to let Aaron and his team take over our Ad account to continue the growth and have since worked together on a hand full of other projects. I would highly recommend anyone who is thinking about working with Aaron to give it a go.

George Sapey, 7 Days Performance

I met Aaron Branch at a time in my life where I was ready to take the next step. I'd recently left full-time employment to pursue my goal as a fully-fledged entrepreneur, and grow my social media marketing agency to new levels.

I had never heard of Aaron before, when I attended the millennial marketing mastery in June 2019, co-hosted with Jordan Platten.

It sounds super cliche, but as soon as I saw Aaron, and spoke with him, I instantly received a new level of energy, and I knew I had to get as close to him as I could.

I soon found out that he was opening up a handful of places on his personal mentorship programme. I knew I had to be on it, there was no question about it.

Over the first 3 months, I became truly overwhelmed with how willingly Aaron supported me throughout the next phase of my business journey. The attention to detail, the resources, the constant check-ins, the personalized feedback. Aaron literally took me by the scruff of the neck and showed me how to structure my business. How to align my personality to be primed for success, and express my inner beast mode, to ensure I got everything I wanted and deserved from my entrepreneurial efforts.

There's a certain aura and energy around Aaron, that you can only feel when you get close to him, and if you do get close to him, you begin to pick things up really quickly. Levels of eye contact, voice tonalities, body language, reactional choice of words. These types of things can't be taught, they can only be observed and adopted. They've fundamentally enabled me to level up my business, level up my life, and dominate my competition.

If I could summarise Aaron Branch in a few sentences (if that was possible) I'd say he has taught me how to be ruthless in business, to develop laser focus on what matters, and eliminate what doesn't.

Sam Modlinsky